Our Imaginary Childhood

poems by

Sara Watson

Finishing Line Press
Georgetown, Kentucky

Our Imaginary Childhood

Copyright © 2023 by Sara Watson
ISBN 979-8-88838-186-1 First Edition
All rights reserved under International and Pan-American Copyright Conventions. No part of this book may be reproduced in any manner whatsoever without written permission from the publisher, except in the case of brief quotations embodied in critical articles and reviews.

ACKNOWLEDGMENTS

Thank you to *PANK* and *The Southern Review*, in which some of these poems previously appeared.

I am grateful to *The Cincinnati Review*, to the University of Cincinnati, and, in particular, to early readers of these poems, whose enthusiasm gave me permission to keep writing them: Brian Brodeur, Jim Cummins, Danielle Deulen, Tasha Golden, Julia Koets, Dave Neilson, Amy Ninneman, Michael Peterson, Linwood Rumney, and Lisa Summe. Thank you, Emily, for the beautiful cover art. Thank you, Stephanie. Thank you, Mitch and Cooper. Thank you to my UC family: Lindsey, Julia, Tiny, Dolores, Janine, Rachael, Mercedes, Bhumika, and Niven. And to my current one: Heather—were I not still desparate to impress you, I may never have sent this book out—Cindy Leah, Soso, and Cora.

Thank you, Mom and Dad and Randy and Jack. And to all the family who drifted in and out along the way.

Publisher: Leah Huete de Maines
Editor: Christen Kincaid
Cover Art: Eoley Mulally
Author Photo: Sara Watson
Cover Design: Elizabeth Maines McCleavy

Order online: www.finishinglinepress.com
also available on amazon.com

Author inquiries and mail orders:
Finishing Line Press
PO Box 1626
Georgetown, Kentucky 40324
USA

Table of Contents

There were eleven of us 1

River won't eat animals 2

We had to get rid of the puppy 3

Graycat had kittens 4

When Sophie eats popcorn 5

When Dahlia wants to be alone 6

Jack practices zero gravity 7

Ruby was born 8

Kid and Honey 9

Maryjane collects bits of blue 10

There are three different paths 11

We got in trouble 12

Ruby has eleven words 13

Maryjane isn't the oldest 14

Dahlia came home 15

This is my favorite ghost story 16

Kid turned 13 on the 13th 17

It must have been a bear 18

In a coffee can marked River 19

Kid has secrets too 20

Every family needs a storyteller 21

You can be good and bad 22

Dahlia likes Little Red Riding Hood 23

*for Aubrey Rose
and for Jack, who was there*

There are eleven of us altogether: Winnie, River, Mary Jane, Dahlia, Honey, Ruby, Sofie, Izzy, Kid, Jack, and me. We sleep in a pile like puppies. Each night we dream the same dream, wherein one of us declares her love for the others. In the morning, nobody can quite remember just who had said just what. Our parents spend whole days in bed. We bring them aspirins and glasses of water, buttered toast cut on the diagonal. They love us, but they have headaches. What we learn from them is this: to never be sorry for anything.

River won't eat animals because of how their eyes look and I like that about her. Jack won't eat anything orange except oranges and our dad says that's right. Try feeding either of them a carrot. You just can't. All of us like licking peanut butter off a spoon, but our mother says rinsing spoons is the *absolute very worst chore ever.* Clean spoons are impossible to find here.

We had to get rid of the puppy. A fluffy white thing so much like a toy, Winnie could not understand its aliveness. *What kind of animal are you?* she'd ask, rubbing the puppy all over her face. Twice, she dropped it off the back porch. Three times she threw it at Izzy. Our parents gave the puppy to someone else's daughter. They said it was the right thing to do.

Graycat had kittens under the house. We name all of them after blue things: Blue Jay, Blue Ribbon, Blue Velvet, Blue Sky, Blue Crayon, Blue Kool-Aid, Blue Window, Blue Eye.

When Sophie eats popcorn, Izzy fills two glasses of water. One to share with Sophie and one for our mother, who wakes up thirsty no matter what time it is. Sophie and Izzy came out of our mother holding hands. That's what River told us. River says Sophie and Izzy rode piggyback inside our mother, then came out to sleep back to back in their crib, each of them sucking a red thumb. They still sleep like that.

When Dahlia wants to be alone she walks back the path to the targets, to where our dad buried the turtle. What she likes is to spell her name there out of stuff she finds around, pebbles and dandelions and dead bees from the windowsill. Like it's *her* grave. Like *she's* buried there. Then she curls up on the grass for a while and pretends to be an only child and an orphan. She likes the sound of the creek running by. The sound of nobody talking.

Jack practices zero gravity in the bathtub. Because our parents cannot afford space camp, even though they think Jack's the smartest. Jack says we can't go to space; we're just in it. Most of the stars are dead, but don't tell Honey. *This here*, says Jack. *This is an Earth rock.*

Ruby was born on the first day of summer. Our mother was so happy to get Ruby out of her she drank a beer right in the hospital. River saw it. For a while our parents didn't know what to name her so her bracelet just said *Baby Girl*. When she wouldn't stop screaming they called her Ruby. River says our mother craved tomato sandwiches and that's why Ruby came out so red. Ruby hates this story.

Kid and Honey roll a tire downhill. Winnie curls up inside, landing in the creekbed with a wet kerplunk. Not even on a dare, just because they told her to. Later our parents make a fire in the backyard and watch our tire burn, sipping whiskey and listening to the radio. We take turns peeking at them out the window. They look very happy.

Mary Jane collects bits of blue eggshell from the edge of the lawn. She's not sure how it works. She's never seen a bird that small. She lines up the shells on the porch railing for the cats to eat, even though Dahlia says it's morbid. She writes a poem in blue chalk on the playhouse floor: *The word home points in every direction.* Mary Jane learned poetry from watching *Reading Rainbow*. She likes everything about that show but the song.

There are three different paths to the kingdom, in case any of them's got a snake across it. Some snakes we are not afraid of. Other ones we turn around for. The kingdom is a fallen tree, a graveyard, a mailbox, and a crow's nest. Some of us spend a lot of time there. Some of us would rather watch tv.

We got in trouble. Because somebody threw out all the cigarettes. Because somebody wouldn't confess, and because everybody hates a tattletale, especially our mother. So we spent the whole day inside with nothing to draw on but the soft parts of each others' bodies. Mary Jane drew the kittens, the twins drew each other, and Ruby draws a heart every time. Winnie, Kid, Honey, Jack and I stood on our heads until our faces were all filled with blood. River snuck out. Dahlia played dead.

Ruby has eleven words for "I don't want to": *sorry, busy, later, never, can't, why, quiet, maybe, mom!, yuck,* and *no.* She has one word for danger and it's *bear.*

Mary Jane isn't the oldest. She doesn't want to grow up fast and move away. She doesn't want to let go of Dahlia's hand, ever. But Dahlia likes to be alone. And Dahlia wants to get away from the cats and the babies and the never-ending keg parties of our parents. So Dahlia packs a sandwich and an apple and a change of clothes. And Mary Jane tucks a love note into the pocket of Dahlia's favorite sweater. Our parents nap on the sofa in the middle of the hot afternoon. Kittens yowl underneath the dining room.

Dahlia came home but our mother did not. Honey has a stomachache, so our dad rubs her belly for hours. Jack pours ginger ale. Dahlia sits next to them eating all of the crackers. The rest of us lie on the floor in front of the tv, our sharp little forearms for pillows. We watch *Dark Shadows* through the space between our fingers. We bite each other's necks.

This is my favorite ghost story—the one where she makes him promise every single night how to bury her. I like the version where he isn't greedy he just misses her too much. The one where he's so sad he loses everything. Because even when he robs her grave he can't just sell the thing, has to live with it under his pillow and the wind howling *Who stole my golden arm?* My favorite part is how the wind sounds exactly like her voice. My favorite part is when he gets his wish at the end.

Kid turned 13 on the 13th of February. It was a Friday. We did the usual thing where we granted his every wish. Mostly we microwaved marshmallows and took turns stirring up milkshakes, made up stories where Kid rescued our mother from inside the belly of a bear. Ruby refused to participate, still upset that at school all the summer birthdays share a party. Ruby was born in June.

It must have been a bear that ate the jack-o-lanterns, the way it must have been an owl that carried off Sophie's favorite cat. A bear leaves a mess. A scatter of birdseed and garbage. The kitty though just disappeared. Like she was never even there.

In a coffee can marked *River*, River keeps the following things: Fawn's collar, nine half-burned birthday candles, the spare key to Dad's truck, an itty-bitty skull, cigarette butts, and a sandwich bag of photos from the day Sophie & Izzy were born (everyone smiling).

Kid has secrets too. He knows the best spots to dig night crawlers, how to bait a hook, and how the babies' bunny got away. He knows where Dahlia hides her cigarettes, and the things she would do to him if he told. He knows our mother wasn't swallowed by a bear.

Every family needs a storyteller, otherwise the family is a secret. Like a glass eyeball buried in the sandbox. Nobody can know what it means. Our dad says a story is like a hot drink on a cold day. It thaws you out some. River thinks she's our storyteller. I'm pretty sure that I am.

You can be good and bad at the same time. Like our mother, who is bad because some nights she doesn't come home, and now she's been gone a long time. But she's good because she loves us and pets us and makes us take baths and doesn't make us do much else. Bad at checking homework but good at braiding hair. Good at dancing. Not so good at getting out of bed.

Dahlia likes Little Red Riding Hood because of the ending, when the granny is found alive still inside the wolf. For a long time she carried a basket wherever she went. But I like Hansel and Gretel because they're brother and sister. I like to imagine a house all made of candy. A trail made of breadcrumbs. And how the witch fattens them up. Maybe their parents left them or sent them away or maybe they were just on an adventure. What we know for sure is that they went along hand in hand. And when the time came they survived together too.

Sara Watson's poems have appeared in *BOAAT, PANK, Rattle, The Southern Review,* and other publications. She received her Ph.D. in English and Comparative Literature from the University of Cincinnati, where she served as Associate Editor of *The Cincinnati Review.* She teaches at the University of Pittsburgh and continues to interrogate class and gender dynamics in her teaching, writing, and living.

www.ingramcontent.com/pod-product-compliance
Lightning Source LLC
Chambersburg PA
CBHW022128090426
42743CB00008B/1052